LOCKDOWN SONNETS - VOLUME II & Other Poems

Pradeep Dharmapalan

BookLeaf Publishing
India | USA | UK

Presentation by *BookLeaf Publishing*

Web: www.bookleafpub.com

E-mail: info@bookleafpub.com

ISBN: 9789363316072

First edition 2024

Dedicated to my parents

K. G. Dharmapalan and Parvathy Dharmapalan

Lockdown Sonnets
Volume II

I

flattery was once enough
to lower all defences
an embarrassed cough
to waive all offences

now it's not so simple
to wriggle swiftly in
or appear as a pimple
on the smoothest skin

but it comes at a cost
a price has to be paid
till everything is lost
lights altogether fade

•

in solitude, to ponder
and unclean linen launder

kolkata: 14 april 2020

II

poet of the people, poet of passion
voice of the tongue-tied and inarticulate
so very long dead, but always in fashion
leaving several generations forever in debt

with animal energy, primal urges and desires
like a mighty bird, in the heavens, he soars
removing all impurities with his raging fires
with roaring tempests, breaking down all doors

with leopards' gums, all pink, and tigers' tails
he paints raw emotion with rare intensity
and, into the tossing waves, intrepidly sails
for a timeless tryst with sweet serendipity

ah pablo, how could mere poison have killed you?
you made gold of base metals, diamonds of dew

kolkata: 14 april 2020

III

everyone, i'm sure, can think of happier times
especially at this moment of collective gloom
when the pressure, of relenting, shows no signs
and a country clumsily braces to combat doom

a new year begins for many millions this day
known by different names in different parts
but the usual festivities are nowhere on display
and it is not joy today that fills people's hearts

further testing times have been announced
wearied minds have been replenished with dread
decisions are hailed and decisions denounced
and upward climb global numbers of the dead

what we anxiously ask, happens next?
to the glorious narrative, the stirring sub-text

kolkata: 14 april 2020

HOUSE ROOMS
FOR STAY

IV

the mind must, perforce, freely roam and wander
it cannot remain chained to one person or place
time is precious, and cannot be blithely squandered
as before us loom, so large, disaster and disgrace

when the body is, to a limited space, for days confined
a toxic unease builds up, and through the being spreads
seeping into the soul, and contaminating the mind
emptying the heart of happiness and filling it with dread

the mind travels wide and far, alights on myriad things
and, in so doing, keeps the crucial spark in us alive
helps us to rise from dark depths, spread our wings
and grants the courage to seek, struggle and strive

no walls ever built, have contained the human mind
be bold and be brave—seek and you shall find

kolkata: 14 april 2020

V

i probably would not have pleased shams tabrizi
with my ambivalent position on love and living
but his prescriptions, to follow, are not that easy
beyond the transactional basis of taking and giving

love has always been important, crucially so, in fact
but has been wrapped around the self, nourishing
the soul within, providing the strength needed to act
and produce these works, this industry flourishing

if anything, i've been like the moor, guilty of excess
loving injudiciously, extravagantly, but selfishly, too
leaving all doors open, offering free and easy access
always doing what i wished, and not what i ought to

but i do dance wildly, have robes that swirl and swish
and, in the eyes of the uninitiated, could pass for a
dervish

kolkata: 14 april 2020

VI

with hat, mask, cape and sword
he cuts, in black, a very sharp figure
and although he often seems bored
can out-swish the quickest trigger

no one knows who he really is
his name, background or intentions
but he brings to dullness a little fizz
and other delights no one mentions

music in smoke-filled rooms, loud laughter
the babble of the obtuse and ill-informed
he is there, but no one knows what he's after
sticking out in the crowd, outlandishly uniformed

if only, he thinks, they would have me unmasked
i could give them the answer that no question asked

kolkata: 16 april 2020

VII

there is more to life than what meets the eye
our senses perceive but a miniscule fraction
unimaginable horizons stretch far beyond the sky
and we do not even get to see a piece of that action

like planets around stars, we have orbits, too
and spend our lives moving in chosen grooves
to destinations we would perhaps never go to
if it were we who actually made these moves

random events, claim atheists, denying a plan
god's will and grace, cry believers, piously bowed
two extremes of the limited mental range of man
within which we exist, lost in the teeming crowd

the current moves, and we move with it
mindless minions spewing glorious bullshit

kolkata: 17 april 2020

SAFE DRIVE
SAVE LIFE
BIDHANNAGAR CITY POLICE

VIII

should have known better, mrs. superman couldn't
help thinking
than to marry a man with superhuman strength and
other assorted powers
hero to the world, he left his wife alone at home, at
the sink, sinking
trying to swim through dark waters, as outside fell
fresh april showers

days were always too short, to fill with everything at
hand to be addressed
and there were always more important matters, urgent
and pressing
what hope had she of laughing happily, lying in bed,
both suitably undressed
putting time and the world on 'pause', simple joys,
finding, expressing

he'd never spend more time with her than he did with
villains and bad guys
his responsibility to the world would always come
first, dwarf his to her
volcanos, landslides and earthquakes would always
trump her cakes and pies
and consolation prizes are no consolation, and no
particular glory really confer

for she knew, that while doing super-heroic things
he often quietly broke wind beneath his wings

kolkata: 17 april 2020

IX

since death is widely being discussed
with more seriousness than disgust
it is perhaps an opportune moment
or, for that matter, possibly god-sent

to join the conversation, say a few words
since nothing today can be called absurd
old categories and rules lie rudely shattered
and everything else that seemingly mattered

this is no time to be coy or stupid or shy
it's time to quietly lie down and die
and if asked to provide a fitting epitaph
i'll offer two sentences, no paragraph

'after decades of babbling, he has finally passed
and, the gods be praised, shut up at last'

kolkata: 17 april 2020

DHANTERAS
Shagun
OFFERS
EV CAR

X

we should have known better
but knowing made no difference
we blundered on, fuelled by folly
with passion, greeting indifference

how we plummeted in our own eyes
leaving not a shred of self-respect
knowing, declarations of love apart
there was sweet fuck all to expect

the irony of it all was not lost upon us
such great possibilities cruelly wasted
deadly poison, deliberately transferred
onto lips, which, once, of honey tasted

children and parents to think of, hearts that bleed
souls wrestling, night and day, with demon seeds

kolkata: 19 april 2020

CHEMISTS &

XI

as steven pinker once pointed out
these are the most peaceful times
we enjoyed them, moved freely about
and settled into brand-new paradigms

but unrest, uncertainty and unease
are the oldest companions of the race
corollaries to war, famine and disease
with which we've testily shared space

the second world war lasted six years
routines rudely disrupted, as millions died
but life continued through pain and tears
we hung on till we reached the other side

the ride will be rough, but we will get there
like drowning men rescued, gasping for air

kolkata: 20 april 2020

মেডিকেল ইনস্টিটিউট
DURGA
PUJA

XII

i'm not sure where the boys have gone
maybe they're tired, have had their fill
and run out of word-costumes to don
unable, like others, to produce at will

there was always a line only a few crossed
although pretenders milled merrily about
flinging measly crumbs, into a salad tossed
finding silly reasons to scream and shout

but the picnic is over, the plastic plates flung
into bulging garbage bags, resembling men
filled to the brim with unmedicinable dung
strutting about, like roosters looking for hens

not all trees grow tall or bear succulent fruit
most are charred, leafless and covered in soot

kolkata: 20 april 2020

XIII

the comfortable complain of discomfort
while the miserable in misery die
all principles have the value of sheer dirt
the stench rises all the way to the sky

everyone is affected, that no one denies
we've all been thrown into the mix
but the starving millions are fed only lies
their travails reduced to mere statistics

many people care and strive to assist
those who should, stand around and watch
claiming that they too must idly exist
with everything of value hidden in the crotch

of what use is our culture, of what use, our art?
of what use are lofty ideas, when there is no heart?

kolkata: 20 april 2020

XIV

death had once come to visit me
accompanying cancer, on a social call
but i pretended, at home, not to be
and though i tripped, i did not fall

since then life has continued as before
but i still remember that face
that figure standing silently at the door
to rob me of dignity and grace

he still lurks in hallways and on streets
waiting to quietly whisk me away
he does not think of victories or defeats
nor of clever things to say

it's just his job, something he does
for a paltry salary, and a tiny buzz

kolkata: 20 april 2020

XV

dogs, in general, are more human than many people
i've met
they're warm, loyal, friendly, great listeners and
companions
they may be called animals, walk on all fours, and
bark, yet
are more worthy of our admiration and respect, in my
opinion

than many a murderous human, greedy, callous,
unscrupulous
thinking only of themselves and their own profit,
benefit and gain
unmoved by the plight of others less fortunate,
wholly oblivious
to the fact that they could play a part in reducing
sadness and pain

dogs do this instinctively, without even being asked
to try
constant, consistent, they are steadfast, committed
and true
they will follow you into the jaws of death, without
asking why
and are unswayed by alternatives or the lure of things
new

i salute the considerate canine, man's best friend
and promise to chase my own tail, till the very end

kolkata: 20 april 2020

XVI

there are intricate connections we cannot imagine or
see
reigning rules that we do not understand or even
know
the belief that humans command and control is a
fallacy
we are but nameless bit players in a grand cosmic
show

our feeble minds, ravenous appetites and short
memories
add to the mix, further ingredients to create confusion
we are caught by surprise by the repetition of our
histories
and fail to assimilate knowledge, despite the
profusion

we find ourselves in the same situations, time and
again
suddenly awakening to our frailties and failings
galore
and belatedly wax with dubious eloquence of now
and then
before rushing, post-crisis, our default settings to
restore

so move with the times, go with the flow
don't bother wondering, you'll never know

kolkata: 20 april 2020

XVII

age is often more than just a number, despite what is
said
perspectives depend on how far down the road you
are
while you still think and feel like a teenager inside
the head
the shadows have lengthened, out peeps the evening
star

for once, in this virus-ravaged, bewildered, embattled
world
with rows of rubble and debris to pick from, to
slowly rebuild
age is better suited to negotiate the slings and arrows
hurled
to walk forward without hesitation, unafraid of
getting killed

pity the youth, awoken from a technological trance,
to face
the horror of analog viruses and crippling changes to
lifestyle
thrown into a world that demands rebooting at a
painful pace
recalibration of values and priorities, and masks to
hide smiles

to embrace uncertainty, at that moment, what a joy to
be felt!
to wrestle and writhe and into a pool of molten
passion melt

kolkata: 21 april 2020

XVIII

so you think you can read me from what i've written
and know me from what i've chosen to show
but perhaps you cannot chew all that you've bitten
maybe you don't know all you think you know

there are matters about which i've made no mention
several aspects of myself that i will never reveal
like the power of dark matter that avoids attention
which nature, in its wisdom, chooses to conceal

each blow suffered, each wound sustained, on the
way
has been a lesson learnt, a source of new strength
words and weapons no longer hold their former sway
at the gang-plank's end, having walked the length

barbs and bombs bounce off the skin, i smile
lacking in ceremony, perhaps, but never in style

kolkata: 22 april 2020

XIX

your son is an old man now, not a little boy
inching towards sixty, but not quite there
he still thinks he's an adolescent and enjoys
waltzing, without, in the world, a single care

you no longer watch him with that quiet pride
although he thinks of each of you everyday
he carries you in his heart, lovingly, deep inside
and for your eternal peace, he daily prays

how long is a length of string? who truly knows?
you yourselves were long ago to ashes reduced
he continues to ruffle feathers and tread on toes
and to lengthen the list of hearts he's seduced

but today, in isolation, he will look up at the sky
think of happy times with you, then gently sigh

kolkata: 22 april 2020

XX

another day goes by
evening deepens into night
irony, absurdity
light in search of light

another year goes by
air captured in standard cages
unit upon unit, growing
the process unfolds in stages

another lifetime goes by
like countless millions before
unheralded, unsung, into oblivion
marching to a stirring score

in a colourful riot, gaudy and bright
to vanish suddenly from all sight

kolkata: 23 april 2020

XXI

in faraway wayanad, my forest home
creatures, great and small, freely move
through the tall trees, wild animals roam
self-assured, their feet in guiding grooves

it is fitting and fair that they are unfettered
and have not met the aboriginals' tragic fate
relying on instincts that lead the unlettered
they know when not to halt, when to wait

it was i who blundered into their world
(not, even for a moment, the other way round)
seeking only to blend, in a corner, quietly curl
to watch nature at work, find the unfound

to sift through layers of pleasure and pain
for a glimpse of the magic in the mundane

kolkata: 23 april 2020

FREE ENTRY

XXII

in the great rush that was called life
(till, at least, the day before yesterday)
We were swept away by stress and strife
with no time to reflect, and nothing to say

but it was there for the discerning to see
even then, through fine cracks, appearing
little stars in the dark, of great luminosity
emissaries from another realm, endearing

we do not know what the future holds
and have, over events, no real control
but poets slip skilfully into silken folds
open unseen vistas of the waiting soul

come, take a closer look at reality
dance with me

kolkata: 24 april 2020

XXIII

rhyme, to many, is dated, anachronistic
out of step with the beating heart
but one is neither reluctant nor apologetic
regardless of convention, art is art

add to that the choice of the sonnet form
and the self-imposed constraints are obvious
as is the pleasure of challenging the norm
without splashing in puddles of the odious

the demands of discipline, fitting into a mould
lend a tightness and sharpness often missed
and open doors into ages, forgotten, old
where, under starlit skies, wind-kissed

we wandered into poetry's core
walking along a nameless shore

kolkata: 25 april 2020

XXIV

it would be so simple to play the victim
cover himself in self-pity and loudly cry
of injustices and crimes, gory and grim
and, amid the debris, curl up and die

but, this is no ordinary whipping boy
who, against a vile onslaught, crumbles
there is sadness, not an ounce of joy
lightning flashes, dark clouds rumble

he stoically bears all, chooses not to retaliate
being pragmatic enough to gauge the mood
thinking it petty to challenge a debt so great
works, pride ignored, towards a greater good

in the search for the sacred, the quest for the pure
there is hardship to experience, ugliness to endure

kolkata : 25 april 2020

XXV

everyone's mad, in their way
lunatics, one and all
lashing out, night and day
backs against the wall

with preposterous beliefs
and blind faith
lost in tea-leaves
and red tape

you can't take sides
everyone is right
taking you for rides
through the night

madness prevails, madness rules
on tossing waves, a ship of fools

kolkata: 25 april 2020

XXVI

it is the acceptance of facts, not courage
that we have needed every single day
to continue to perform on the world-stage
and learn to deflect feeling deftly away

it could, easily, have been so different
had minds been more mature and fair
but, quickly, down the drain it all went
all hopes extinguished for want of air

overlapping chapters were never written
stories radically separate trajectories took
multiply shy, countless times being bitten
there was no dialogue in much of the book

in which each of us play our part
on the same planet, worlds apart

kolkata: 26 april 2020

Coca

XXVII

the irony is that one hasn't been selfish
or made callous and uncaring choices
stopped others from thinking as they wish
or even engaged with discordant voices

no one wants to be second best, one understands
nor wishes to share the spoils with another
that's the way we are, obeying inner commands
all other considerations choosing to smother

in an atmosphere of toxic disbelief, little takes root
sincerity and goodwill are entirely wasted
once gleaming objectives, now all covered in soot
are forgotten with the joys once tasted

the lessons are not new, nor are the insights
everything seems so small, from these heights

kolkata: 27 april 2020

XXVIII

it is fitting, some would be tempted to say
poetic justice, o what delicious irony
never known to be kind on any given day
looking for support, won't find any

they madly fling whatever they can at me
try, ridiculously, to settle silly scores
use all that they can think of: lies, calumny
and the sort of garbage one abhors

all the fine feelings we professed to cherish
have mysteriously dissipated with time
we watch everything we loved now perish
and i've only got myself left to call mine

as the sun, off wet leaves, after april showers
shines on scattered petals of withered flowers

kolkata: 27 april 2020

XXIX

they are all the same, for all their claims
made of the same shapeless clay
petty, stupid, looking for things to blame
with nothing significant to say

they presume they are clever, even wise
their self-importance is a pitiful joke
their faces show through every disguise
they are crushed by their own yoke

they sadly mistake kindness for weakness
restraint for the lack of a response
unaware that this atmosphere of bleakness
captures no one but pathetic pawns

kings stride across battlefields, bloodied, unbowed
untouched by mayhem, to an abode in the clouds

kolkata: 27 april 2020

XXX

it is so difficult to be understood
preconceived notions lie littered
all over the path, intentions good
on the road to hell, sadly frittered

after all, it is no longer about winning
or losing, it is about closing, gracefully
fireworks were welcome in the beginning
but farewells are best said peacefully

it is possible life is not entirely over as yet
there could still be much in store
and one need not look sadly at the sunset
there are likely to be many more

ah solitude, i've missed the silken caress
the passion, the sensuality, the finesse

kolkata: 27 april 2020

XXXI

everyone is full of insights these days
wisdom is pouring out of their ears
but no one listens to what another says
or has the time to wipe others' tears

nothing can compare with a good crisis
to bring out the best and worst in man
a tremendous surge, of virtues and vices
doing the things only homo sapiens can

makes you wonder, how we reached this far
or how we call ourselves intelligent beings
when you can clearly see how stupid we are
visually-challenged, claiming to be all-seeing

truth is, nothing's new, things were always surreal
we just didn't have the time to watch them congeal

kolkata: 29 april 2020

Fairy Tales for the Times

01

addressing the ornate, image-reflecting, adornment
hanging on the wall, queenie-baby, big daddy's new
missus
wonders whose appearance sets every man's pants on
fire
who is the true object of passionate desire
hoping—no, praying—the answer will be
that it is she

so, she isn't exactly amused, when the mirror
looking slightly confused, says, shaking its head
sorry, lady, it's not you tonight
it's your step-daughter, willowy, snow white

she has the defective mirror removed at once, and
replaced
with one that gives only one answer—the right one,
obviously—each time
it's asked.

as for the step-daughter, she's never seen, or heard
from, ever again
despite rumours of seven diminutive men, with
ridiculous names
desperately in need of a decent shit, shower and
shave

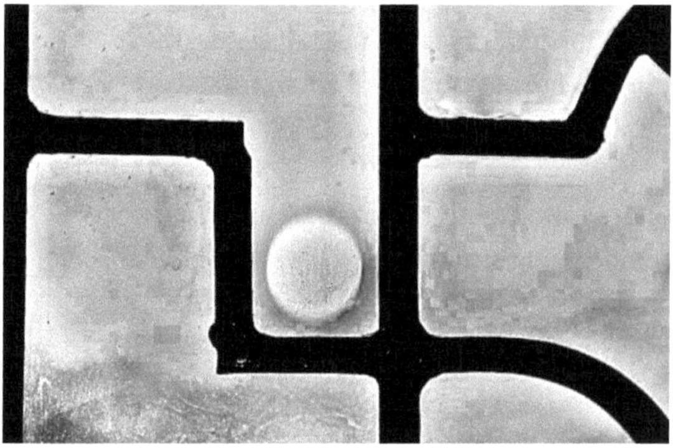

02

two of the trio of porcine siblings—who gained a degree of fame
for their part in bringing to book the errant wolf
who, with halitosis, had subjugated an entire fringe community
of animals, great and small—believed they owed their success
to the more studious and industrious third
whose knowledge and craftsmanship
had fashioned the stone and brick shelter
the wolf failed to penetrate with gusts of vile vapour
but when a runaway elephant came along
and, with a swing of his trunk and a few lusty kicks
knocked their homestead down
they were quick to clarify what they meant
was that no solution is lasting
and no victory permanent

PANAMA TEA CO.

03

as the name—little red riding hood—immediately
tells you
the child's parents were not the most imaginative,
intelligent or responsible
who else names their child after an insignificant piece
of apparel?
as if names like julie or sophie or mary were no
longer available
or were too expensive for folk like themselves
who else stays home to party with like-minded
buddies
and sends a child, laden with a basket of food,
through a forest
to fulfill a filial obligation to a parent they couldn't
be bothered
to visit themselves or even ring, given that
technology moves ahead
in tales of this kind, but human nature remains
unchanged
little wonder then, that the wolf, having given up an
interest in ham
met a perfect match in the grandmother, whose brief
marriage
had been largely unsatisfying, and, contrary to
reports, circulated
by danish journalists seeking to proclaim the glories
of inexpensive speech
the grandmother is still alive and is deliriously happy,
the wolf
has found a cure for his issues of breath, and the child

having despatched her parents to prison for their
woeful parenting skills
now lives with her boyfriend in a house down the
lane
and was last seen in a shop, looking to buy a name

04

mrs bear, being, like most wives, the more sensible and sensitive
of the marital duo, had felt a strange uneasiness for some time
something was not quite right

was it her husband? she had wondered
it didn't appear to be, he was going through each day
at his own wheezing pace, fumbling, stumbling, tumbling
through life
junior? she had thought
but what he could do
that could be a cause for worry?
he was eating and sleeping well
and his grades were good, too
they had even bought him an ipad
to show him how happy they were with him

the ipad! of course, the ipad!
contact with far-distant worlds and all kinds
of creatures, familiar and strange, like this woman
with ruddy cheeks and soft, golden curls
lying, unabashedly, in her son's bed
telling her how much she loved her darling ted

05

anyone who has grown their hair longer than an inch
will tell you that it's bloody hard work maintaining a flowing mane
all the brushing and washing, the shampoos and conditioners,
the constant grooming wears you out, and you have to carry it around
like an inert serpent siamese twin, forever falling and getting tangled up
in impossible knots, but few know that the lady with the endless tresses
leading a solitary existence in a tower on the forest's edge
is, in fact, from gaza and had arrived in this land seeking asylum
fleeing the harsh realities netanyahu and his cohorts had introduced
so it was not a fashion statement she was trying to make with her locks
nor indeed a political one, for they tend to be uttered as part
of an orchestrated chorus, no, like another gazan of an earlier age
who was to wander eyeless, courtesy his wife's treachery and sharp scissors
her strength lay in her tresses, her tenacity that of the roots that clung
to her scalp for dear life, unlike the sightless,
perishing, wordlessly, under the noonday sun

06

no one, not even an ant, likes to be called small
and you can imagine how happy i was at being called little
but there's not much you can do about most things in life
you have to wordlessly take the rough and pray
that the smooth will soon arrive someday
and, in the meantime, just get on with it

although later events were to prove it a false alarm
i was well within my rights to express my concern
and run from house to house and person to person
to warn everyone of the imminent collapse of the world's ceiling
and any order that humans sought to impose
on nature and other life forms
the sky—clouds and birds and aircraft and all —was
from its lofty perch about to fall
as was predicted by the furies and the fates
and seconded by vitalstatistix the gaul

07

having seen what her fairy godmother could do
with a pumpkin and a few mice, ella knew
that much more could come her way than
an invitation to the royal ball
her stepmother and step-sisters might call
the shots, but hot they were not
and she positively sizzled in her short, sequined dress
causing in the pimply princeling great distress
as a rush of bubbling blue blood
assailed his vacant head
the rest is pointless conjecture, as we all now know
that she manipulated events thereafter, with that glass shoe
and, a fortune, later made
as brand ambassador for jimmy choo

08

apart from the odd, size-specific role
in movies such as ‘honey, i shrank the kids’
thumbelina did not make much of a headway
in the world of show biz and entertainment
they might say that small is beautiful, but they don’t mean it
and beyond a point, it’s all bullshit, anyway
men have only one thing on their minds
and she was in no position to oblige
so she decided to return to nature, and the half-open buds
that were hers to sleep in, the crystal droplets of dew
that quenched her thirst, and there, among the stalks and leaves
among the flowers and trees, she saw that her hopes and aspirations
practically her entire life, were torn completely to tatters
and with a mighty and miniscule sense of regret, realized that
contrary to the protestations of the righteous, size indeed matters

09

since may last year, jack had begun to notice a
change
in the demeanour of his cows, an air of haughty
disdain
now hung over their usually benign countenances
and they often ignored his commands
as if they now held the upper hand

not one inclined to go to battle against cattle
jack swiftly marched his herd to the market
and in a dazzling act of going green
sold them all for a bag of beans

his mother, tired of his erratic and obtusely idealistic
behaviour
had decided that she could take no more
and walked out of the non-existent door, before he
returned
unfazed, he set up an organic farm
and there now toils day and night, with boundless
energy and love
on soil turned golden by the dropping turds
falling from the giant's castle, in the clouds above

10

questions, of course, will be raised about notions of beauty
and the prejudices that these, and the makers of beauty products
encourage and support, dispatching many into starry-eyed pursuit on a rainbow
of lotions, creams and perfumes, and others into a spiral of depression from which
they never successfully emerge

more importantly, geneticists do not appear to be able to agree
whether this sort of spontaneous mutation can take place in duck embryos
or whether—and this is where a moral dimension is added—that the mother duck
had been impregnated by a swan—zeus, perhaps—in a rehash of the leda episode
or one of his retinue, enjoying a bit of sport, ruffling a few feathers

the duckling itself, now well on its way to becoming a swan
practices new neck movements every day, and is instinctively able to find
answers to questions that never entered its mind

11

hansel should have known better than to accept
grethel's offer of cream of mushroom soup
they were in kodai, and there was that mischievous glint in her eye
but he never paid her much attention of late
he sensed he was changing, but was not sure into what
kafka's metamorphosis gave him nightmares, anil rao's little hope
coloured visions began to enter his thoughts
the world was filled with soothing, resplendent hues
lucy, with her precious stones, led them on and they walked
deep into the forest, leaving the roads and buildings far behind
suddenly, before them stood a house made of the choicest confectionary
cakes and pastries and pies and an entire array of other goodies
made every brick of each wall, each window and door frame,
each rafter and tile,
has concrete gone out of style? hansel asked
smiling, in his mind, from ear to ear, while grethel nibbled at a piece
of black forest window, that had crumbled into her hand, at her touch
that's not probably what you think it is, grethel, cautioned hansel

being, in this matter, somewhat more experienced
than his adopted sister
a fact that she was forced to later admit
while convalescing in a hospital down south
where they were forced to take her
to get the bee stings out of her mouth

12

the piper—ulrich was his name—was a bitter man
he was an artiste, a man with superior skills,
sophisticated tastes
music was his medium, and his goals, lofty and noble
and these wretched people, unscrupulous, selfish and
greedy
had smeared him with allegations so foul and vile
that no perfume produced in this world could the
stench remove
he had offered a non-toxic, pest control option to the
village council
and they, having accepted the terms, reneged once the
job was done
duplicitous sons of unmarried parents, they cheated
him
and needed to be taught a lesson, through the holes of
the pipe
nets of melody went out and caught all the children in
the village
and they dutifully followed him as he walked away
and that was it, nothing else, no more
but to suggest that he had other motives
that he meant the children harm
was so untrue, so untrue
but what can one man do?

mumbai : 24 january 2015

Stray Thoughts
on the
Nature of Things

I

consider, if you will, the facts, as we know them:
a minor rock in space, with other rotating rocks
in revolving orbit, around a ball of flaming fire
a vast ocean of space, too large for our imagination to capture
too complex for our intellect to fully understand
a grand, everlasting pageant, to borrow dostoevsky's phrase
of which we are a small, and perhaps significant, part
of recent advent and indefinite length of stay
so impressed with our own achievements, as to overlook
the true roots of the redwoods, we so admire, of our minds
the reason why we find reasons, where none, perhaps, exists

it is not necessarily our fault, if we focus on the inconsequential
and quench our thirst for answers on drinks, fizzy and coloured
if what we suspect is true—if, indeed, there can be truth—
all we say and do, must follow the self-same script
that speaks through the spiraling strands of dna
which shapes the bodies we live in, the minds with which we dream
propels us headlong into gory battle, or to wrestle between satin sheets

if that is so, and it well could be, and b follows a and c follows b
then all is as it should be, men will squabble, men will die
never be free of the stranglehold of differing inner drives
and never really be in control of our lives

dubai: 09 february 2013

II

that, then, is the premise—or is that too grand a claim to make?
for every strand that is captured or tamed, several others slip away
every utterance on stacks of unstable assumptions rests
and, given the findings of our incomplete science, it is difficult to say
whether matter is a particle or wave or something else all together
there is, in fact, no certainty—and certainly no facts
and all these great heaps of verbiage, that we pile upon ourselves
little more than incoherent babbling, of no real import or substance

but, like everything else we do—eat, sleep, copulate and the rest
we appear duty-bound, dna-driven, to contemplate and give names
to the scraps of knowledge that we pick up along the way
everyone has something to say, to declare and even fight for
and this ability—or disability, as some might say—leads us to believe
that we are superior to other living beings, and the masters of our destinies

but a dispassionate analysis, to the extent our raging
emotions will permit
reveals a different story, written in the dark and
multiple folds of the subconscious
there is a mind within our minds, that calls the shots
from inside

dubai: 09 february 2013

TOTAL

III

what was it, in those early infant years, now forgotten
that stirred, of its own accord, within the nascent
mind
as the body struggled, to understand its limbs and
limits
and a hazy picture, frightening and fascinating
from colours and shapes bewildering, began to form
and physical sensations and the demands of emotions
set to work, sculpting the character, from the given
rock
made of flesh, but miraculously alive, blossoming to
fullness
contending with a world outside, a world within

days, weeks, months, years passed, all tiny grains of
sand
we clambered, repeatedly, onto pedestals, and then
fell
calling it experience and knowledge, as we sought to
find
our place in this vast world and vaster cosmos
relying on received wisdom, the views of those who
preceded us
and through their words of praise and fear, hope and
despair
traced our own confused paths through the
mysterious woods
taking comfort in routine, seeking solace in repetition
eventually settling, like the planets, in elliptical orbits

around fiery questions, globular and bright,
unanswered

dubai: 10 february 2013

ASTHA
Neem

IV

an april morn, delhi's wide, windswept roads
atop a borrowed motorcycle, i rode, the breeze in my hair
a buzz in my head, a song in my heart, issuing from my lips
i took the turns with verve and vigour, and exaggerated flourish
the oncoming bus, labouring up the slope, was spotted too late
as i, intoxicated on youth and other earthly pleasures, swung
into its path, the wide extravagant curve delivering me directly
to a space before its mammoth tyres of burning rubber, screaming death
in the flash of a moment, i suddenly saw, a life ill-understood, come to a close
the indefinite reprieve, the cornerstone of my thought, being draped with specificity

but it was not to be; the shock had stilled the accelerator, slowed the momentum
and i found myself crashing against the bus, not under its murderous wheels
injured and dazed, jeans ripped, motorcycle damaged, i had survived
shaken and stirred from the embrace of the absurd, still very much alive

rising again, the torn seat of my jeans dusted, i
jumped onto the mangled bike
and continued the journey, through the awakening
traffic, down delhi's roads
through the meandering highways and by-lanes of
terrestrial life

dubai: 11 february 2013

Kalam

V

how happy she was, recalling and recounting times gone by
when she travelled, half a century in the past, with her father-in-law
in a horse-cart, through a town of unfamiliar smells, sounds and people
gruff, but kind, he was, momentarily, the father she had lost
as a child, years earlier still, leaving her with a widowed mother
a string of struggling siblings and whimsical uncles to deal with
marriage was no escape—it brought its own chains
a mother-in-law who breathed fire, a husband all of twenty-two
with brothers, young and libidinous, crawling all over the house

it was never an easy life, the vagaries and terrors overwhelmed her
stoically, she held on, believing life, despite all, to be too sacred to end
accepting her lot, wordlessly, as destiny or divine deliverance
and with well-intentioned care, filled her son with all her fears
preaching timidity and submissiveness as the mantra for survival

until, unable to watch the schoolyard bullying he
haplessly endured
asked him to return the blows, passivity discarded,
assertiveness assumed
allowing the confused youngster to steer a course
onto the high seas
where his qualities of head and heart, initially stifled,
found fuller expression

dubai: 12 february 2013

VI

a natural phenomenon, one could say, the consequence
of a marriage of molecules, restless and rampant, seeking completion—
clouds, regal, ethereal, in the grand amphitheatre of the sky
fine wisps of white against the blue, or the large, billowing masses of cumulus
in lumbering march, or grey and angry, of the nimbus tribe, prone to precipitation
or the detached cirrus tails of rabbits, lost in a warren heaven
our minds work, at once, at varying levels, speak in differing tongues
and, ostensibly objective, try to wring every last drop of feeling
from experience, believing the remaining sludge to be the essence
closer to truth, than whoops of joy or the sound of loud wailing
while being driven by great tides of emotion, born in the heart
pumped out to the body's farthest regions, flooding the ticking brain

is it any wonder, then, that we are confused?
or fail to find answers with our tools?
we look in the wrong places, leave questions of significance unasked

and scurry along like furry rodents, in search of elusive prey
with plenty to talk about and nothing to say
pursuing rational ends, in the name of logic and reason
while driven by feeling, controlled by emotion
if life is dna-driven, a lovely set of verses
crafted by a faceless poet, who blesses each atom with the gift of endless song
perhaps there are connections we do not see
and all is exactly as it ought to be

dubai: 13 february 2013

VIII

the science we so greatly revere, that lifted us from our caves and brought us here
places us squarely in the midst of it all, in scale and scope, infinitesimally small
a late arrival, for a brief, fleeting stay, with, in the proceedings, no real say
to go through life like any other creature, our minds the only redeeming feature
and even our minds, which we claim to be free, take us only halfway up the tree
we satisfy ourselves with tiny fragments, and leave the rest to testaments
we eat, sleep, copulate, and turn around to vigorously wipe clean the slate
and, in the quest to, our maker, meet, can only ask questions and accept defeat

that is the point, for some, at which life is found to have truly begun
the ignominy of ignorance, boundless shame, a minor player in a mysterious game
that is the price to be paid, as all hopes of triumph fade
watching the masses mindlessly march, beneath the dome, through the arch
feeling in the melting mood, the cold, clammy fingers of solitude
the mind continues to try and seek, another mind with which to speak

but fails to find the perfection it seeks, blows kisses
across weathered cheeks
and acknowledges it can only feel free, releasing
surging torrents of poetry

dubai: 15 february 2013

IX

it is afternoon; the sun shines brightly still
but has, of warmth, lost a considerable degree
and offers only a benign luminosity
as the birds, at their places of work and play
think of winging their way back home

what shall we make of the meagre gains
from this existential commerce
lessons learned, patterns discerned
couched in the written and spoken word
in the golden cage, strut golden birds

soft morning light, cool morning air
filter through into the lair
dark and musty
reeking with a stench so stale

on the horizon, boats appear
having, at the break of day, set sail
other things being equal—which they never are—
it would be reasonable to believe
that thought is another name for feeling
and passion a synonym for creative energy
the vehicle of evolution
nature's pathway to the stars

passion is the tree, with mighty boughs and branches
and thought its fruit
glistening in the morning light

through a film of gossamer dew
sink your teeth into its succulent flesh
taste passion anew

kozhikode: 16 february 2013

X

it is a world in a hurry, bustling, impatient
speed is of the essence, all else secondary or worse
with ever-quickening and lengthening strides

the thrust of accelerated locomotion
often offers no real advantage
altogether missing, at times, the intended target
with a spectacular burst of velocity

it is not about being faster or being slower
it is not even about what we know
it is not this, not that, nor who gets to bell the cat
it is not what we see, or hope to comprehend
it has no beginning, no conceivable end
a cosmic conundrum, with a vast celestial cast
with time's different strands entwined
future, present, past

how wonderful to gambol down the street
and, at the intersection, yourself, in the crowd
to meet

kozhikode: 17 february 2013

XI

if we were, for a moment, to take scientists literally
the big bang was a moment of unbridled passion
from which a fertilized egg as a zygote sprang
a far more plausible explanation, than others offered
for the universe's birth and its outward expansion
filling the space thus created with body cells
the solar systems and galaxies, that we, awe-struck,
observe
through our fancy, high-powered, telescopes
we live in a large body, living, breathing
our bodies are universes of their own
and so on, endlessly, inward and outward
perfectly reasonable, totally absurd

but the question remains unanswered: what the hell is
going on?
universes with bodies and bodies within bodies,
inform but do not explain
the nature of the contest, the rules and regulations of
the game
for most, there is a user-friendly package of some
shape or form
to provide the stupor of solace, a cloud cover, which
light
rarely penetrates, and in the gathered gloom, to
stumble on furniture
in the living room; for many, it is mindless
wandering, wanton hedonism
and for others still, against all possible odds
it is about justifying the ways of man to god

kochi: 18 february 2013

XII

pilgrims, from wide and far, all walks of life
gather at the temple town, throng its narrow streets
night and day, for a chance to prostrate themselves
at the lord's feet, in the lord's abode
krishna the mischievous, krishna the promiscuous
krishna the philosophizing charioteer
all this is very good, but, pray, what brings you here?

opium of the masses it may well be, but it is also their elixir
and that is a purpose it serves well, giving many an individual
a sense of community, of belonging, indeed, of identity
(the problem, of course, is in identifying with that identity)
if there is a design, and hence a sort of attendant meaning
then all is going per plan and is as it should be
and if there isn't, and chaos rules
who'd worry about meaning, but fools?

kozhikode: 20 february 2013

XIII

life is precious, we are told, yet daily thousands die
caught in the crossfire, or simply destitute,
dispossessed, old
life is precious, because this process, which we, try as
hard as we might
are never able to conclusively comprehend or define,
demands respect
and, therefore, being, of it, a part, our existence is of
some significance
although precisely why and what we are not likely to
ever know
and, if life is precious, as it is so vehemently claimed
then to snuff it out before its unspecified specific
time is done
is wrong, frowned upon, considered reneging on the
deal
which, in practical terms, does not leave much room
for us to calmly sit and contemplate our doom

since care of the body, and catering to its many needs
—food, drink, clothing, shelter, sleep and rest
correct levels of blood pressure and blood sugar—
seems to take most of our terrestrial time, its reduced
capacity
and falling levels of efficiency, should be cause for
alarm
or, at the very least, concern of the serious kind
and, being human, there is also pride, human dignity

a pointless emotion perhaps, but one that makes us stand defiant
and raise a lone voice in the vast arena of time and space
where the questions we are able to ask, become the lasting emblem of our disgrace

kozhikode: 20 february 2013

XIV

not all insects grow into beautiful butterflies
some just bigger insects become, leading dangerous
lives
doing all kinds of hard work, and never
finishing first in beauty pageants in any part of the
world
they are the ones who, with great gusto, play the
cacophonic sounds
that fill the forest night, where humans go seeking
silence
and the peace it purportedly brings
nothing, it would appear, is all of one piece
and an uncle was once accused of courting his niece

truth be told: logic misleads us
like language and grammar
it has imprisoned, not freed, us
the air is rarer in the higher reaches, as are the sights
vistas breathtaking, like a magic carpet rolled out
but the distance is soothing, too, to be removed
from the dust, the din and the dingbats of human
habitation
where minds constantly are at work, to seek
advantage and domination
the never-ending battles, the unceasing war
and the countless lives they claim
leave most wraithlike, rootless and perplexed
with no fixed address, and no real name

kozhikode: 20 february 2013

XV

relative to our size, there is enough happening around
us
to keep our meagre minds feverishly occupied,
finding means and ways
to benefit, ourselves and those we care for, from
far-reaching enterprise
the more energetic, twitching with strength unspent
wait to leap into galvanized action, tearing down
structures
and, with equal facility, putting others in their place
even the contemplative have copious quantities of
cud to consume
ruminating with smug, well-practiced, ease—it was
all old hat
the universe and creation and all that

and amidst all these single-minded—barring the
occasional, brief, detour—
pursuits, this dogged adherence to prescribed lines,
glibly masquerading as choice
sits one who looks beyond the boundary wall, who
sees in each human city
a large colony of ants, in each ant colony, a flurry of
moving molecules
and in each molecule, a solar system, linked to sister
solar systems,
forming an all-pervading, all-absorbing
all-encompassing universe

who hears in every thought, the voice of feeling, and
in the voice of feeling
the clatter of alphabets of dna, clambering up a spiral
staircase—
at that point the hearing stops, the vision fails
and life becomes one long and painful old wives' tale

kozhikode: 21 february 2013

XVI

going by what is sometimes claimed, others know me better than i do
which should not be too difficult, as, to know myself, i do not claim
but it is preposterous, nonetheless, as i am the recipient of first information
and no one sees or hears anything i have not seen or heard before
they can, at best, have the same—but in no event can they have more
it is from perception and interpretation the differences spring
taking contradictory positions, circling each other, like sweaty wrestlers
sizing each other up within the constricted ring, jockstraps drenched and bulging
if one stays, there is no choice, one has, perforce, to fight
if not, one needs to walk out, never to return, into the night

has vision made us go totally blind? it has been blinkered eye-sight, at best
just enough to do the tasks at hand, focus on the here and now
go about our earthly business in the desired manner, be good homo sapiens
but with blinkers removed, an altogether different spectacle awaits you

immense in scale, delicate, intricate, infinite
a load roar, a grand all-encompassing sweep
suddenly, it matters not whether we're living or dead
suddenly, no more needs to be said

kozhikode: 21 february 2013

7044477704
7044477704
SPA
7044477704
SPA
SPA
SPA

XVII

her name was rocky and her brother's el dorado,
that's all i know
or, at least, remember; martin luther king was alive,
bobby kennedy's toothy grin held promise and
vietnam had not become
the nightmare it was going to be; the trees were tall
and leafy, shedding acorns
generously onto the sidewalk, where the children of
the block played
it was a game of hide and seek that found two
four-year-olds, hiding together
in the nook of a basement entrance, hidden, as was
the objective
away from prying eyes, which allowed them to close
theirs
and bring together their lips—an enthralling moment,
sparkling, free
for the hispanic and the indian, on the road to
self-discovery

with every new discovery came knowledge, of the
world and of oneself
initially hesitant, reluctant, timid, one grew gradually
more intrepid
wandering, further and farther away, from the
familiar patch
like a beachcomber, gathering shells, eager to hear
the story each one tells

i moved farther and further, until, pausing to reflect, one day
i found the world was indeed round—i was back on familiar ground
a sense of relieved happiness could not be denied, nor a degree of surprise
but there was also embarrassment and shame, at having lost the most important
game
or at least found wanting, when prowess was most needed
the ignominious existence of the vanquished, defeat having been conceded

kozhikode: 23 february 2013

XVIII

and, pray, what is a cliché, but something you choose
to say
that has been said a million times or more, much,
much before
the words formed in your mouth, and issued forth
from your lips
and, by virtue of that, all language is clichéd, through
repeated use
frayed, tattered, mere rags of expression, no longer
resplendent
no longer a picture of finery and finesse; or do we, as
always
at cross purposes speak, emotions gushing, released
in a moment, weak
declare that meaning, however faded, still retains its
original sheen
but there is a need to be creative with expression, to
experiment with form,
with word patterns, the interplay of person and voice,
the undefined proximate cause
with middle tones and crescendos, with the pregnant
pause

my name? does it really matter? does anything at all
matter?
scratch the surface, a cosmos of swirling atoms
appears, and within each
the story is repeated again and again and again and
again

bills need to be paid, arrangements need to be made
for the winter months and winter years, when the limbs, already stiff
would have more reluctant grown, and the need for lucre to navigate
the inland waterways of societal living, would be greater still
so, it is time, i think, to finally address you, my friends
and introduce myself as the wizard of odds and ends

kozhikode: 24 february 2013

XIX

the absence of a clear, linear, structure—or numbers
that stack neatly up, tallying in all respects, offering
a regular, recognizable, sequence, to rehearse and
repeat—
can be disconcerting, and wobble the steady feet
that carry us, aided by, and against, gravity, upright
in posture, objectives and approach, treating night
as a series of punctuation marks on an unending day,
and day
as an opportunity to strive and seek, work and play
for although our existence is a patchwork quilt of
assumptions
we still finality and certainty, rather irrationally,
demand
as if that was all we require to fully understand

irregular shapes, non-linear forms and other
permutations
subtly balanced, with weight and counterweight
interlocked
are, it would appear, the language of cosmic reality
by framing rules, we make exceptions, by defining
the ordinary
create the extraordinary, become prisoners of the
categories we conjure
but what may sound incoherent may not necessarily
be so
contradictions are not contradictions, unless you
happen to know

that the lines we have drawn around us, are
permanent and real
it would, therefore, be best to unshackle the mind,
and let it run free
across a sun-drenched terrain, lost in a galloping
reverie

kozhikode: 24 february 2013

XX

night: the hum of the refrigerator—punctuated
by a periodic, shudder and rattle—was the only sound
the large house was dark, all lights switched off
the moon, appearing, occasionally, from behind a cloud, passing
brought the wooden banister to brief, radiant, life
as he skipped, soundlessly, down the wide stairway,
armed with distinctions, recently discovered, between natural and social laws
he found her waiting lips, her quivering body, excited, nervous
all vocal expression non-verbal, a ceaseless string of moans, gasps and sighs
sudden giggles, shouts and screams, chocolate and honey, melted ice-cream

like a victorious general of old, surveying the battlefield, littered
with the dead and the dying, and the lucky few, wounded,
but likely to live, he knew that all depended, on any given day,
on how the wind blew, the breeze felt, the gust sounded
and not on superior numbers or strategy, or advantages in arms or intelligence
it was ostensibly a game of chance, this wild dance with fatal consequences

but was probably predetermined, part of the minute
calculations that presumably
support the superstructure we call physical reality,
although it is probably
only a layer of skin, in a massive, multi-layered
onion, potent, pungent
no matter how clever we think we've become, this is
only the age of knowledge, not
wisdom

kozhikode: 25 february 2013

miscellany: 2024

01

the purity of gaze and purpose
the air of innocence and simian gravitas
strip away layers of hominid nurturing
carbon-dating living tissue

and the crackling sparks
in the winding coils of the brain
look outward for answers held within
a second existence inside

a second skin

kozhikode: 13 january 2023

02

a fine place to keep the powder dry
these northern reaches, where warrior clans once reigned
crisp and moisture-free, dried leaves surrender instantly
at the faintest hint of pressure, crumbling to the finest dust—
powder, of course, and oh so dry

anniversaries of death and near-death, strangely
find me clambering up the sides of dormant volcanoes
or the steep ramparts of historic forts, under a merciless sun

as the aravallis rise out of the desert's borders and run
across man-made boundaries, towards the capital

so, in a metal bird through the sky, tomorrow, shall i
to renew old ties, breathe the familiar air of unhappy quality
so much and so little has changed, the same old story
dreams of yesterday and memories of tomorrow
entangled, like knickers in the proverbial twist

jaipur: 27 march 2024

03

ghalib lies buried not far from here
ignored by those swaying to faster beats
but walked the dirty lanes i once walked
and trudged down the same grimy streets

his head, too, must have swum in similar clouds
opaque and porous, a drifting nothingness
and wrestled with questions no answer would unlock
pathos and bathos, all things absurd and ridiculous

moving from one group of friends to another
never staying long enough to test or strain ties
with an ache in his soul and warmth in his heart
a hint of amusement, a touch of wonder, in his eyes

new delhi: 01 april 2024

04

in the muted light of dawn, the river
lying in the middle distance
could be taken for a vast tract of barren land
bare and unrelieved by any features
other than its singular emptiness

a solitary frog, which long years on this planet
allowed me to recognize in the semi-darkness
hops across the lines of tiled-paths
between geometric patches of manicured lawn
his years, however they are measured, playing a silent part
in guiding his course across time and space
hemmed in by a thousand constraints, the checks and balances
that keep the machine, the sum of all humming parts, going
until the insides collapse, and the outside settles into silence

standing on its banks, the river's movement is caught by the searching gaze
its gentle currents, almost imperceptible, move quietly forward
incessant and steady, without anthropomorphic qualities assigned
it possibly serves the same purpose those who presume to describe it do
as they unwittingly live a truth they spend a lifetime failing to find

taki: 22 april 2024

05

as kerala votes, the prodigal floats
on heat waves in other climes
while battle cries and blatant lies

announce troubled times

in another state, a woman waits
her 35th year to greet
the genes are the same, as once was the name
which denial seeks to defeat

these silly pursuits, between roots and fruits
contribute to this bizarre game
lose or win, save or sin
dance with the flickering flame

kolkata: 26 april 2024

06

that moment
when you've just
closed your eyes
and sleep has not
fully arrived

when the mind
turns out the lights
throws off its clothes
and disintegrates
into a million pieces

which everyone knows
but rarely mentions

instinctively favouring
the solidity of the familiar
to the nebulous embrace

of the void

kozhikode: 04 may 2024

07

they awakened me in the middle of the night
with the sounds of their union, long-delayed
as the moisture of the earth, having departed
and travelled far, finally returned, bare and flayed

to reunite, as spirit to the physical self
with the parched being, powdering to dust
having waited long and hot days and nights
destroyed by despair, consumed with lust

a welcome dampness settles, the nostrils tingle
petrichor-fuelled, there's relief and happy brightness
the world's ills, inevitably, remain and continue
but there is room, in the chaos, for lightness

it rained in kozhikode last night, if you will
in fact, it's raining still

kozhikode: 14 may 2024

08

in time, all things mutate
the tender stem
a bark-encased trunk
becomes

the lust for life
in a moment, is snuffed
it's funny, yes
life's tough

but the fruit on the branches
leaf-covered, fanning out
hold the key
to another round

circling around
we reach where we began
walking on the world
that we hold in our hands

kozhikode: 17 july 2024

9 789363 316072

Printed by Libri Plureos GmbH in Hamburg, Germany